MW01126848

Practice in Building Bridges

Companion resource to
Diversity in Early Care and Education, 5th ed.

Intisar Shareef and Janet Gonzalez-Mena

National Association for the Education of Young Children
Washington, DC

Photographs copyright © by: Paula Jorde Bloom–12; Larry Garf–cover photo; William Geiger–34; Barbara Reynolds–20.

National Association for the Education of Young Children
1313 L Street NW, Suite 500
Washington, DC 20005-4101
202-232-8777 or 800-424-2460
www.naeyc.org

Practice in Building Bridges

Copyright © 2008 by the National Association for the Education of Young Children. All rights reserved. Printed in the United States of America. This companion resource to a Special NAEYC Edition of Janet Gonzalez-Mena's *Diversity in Early Care and Education* (McGraw-Hill, 2008) is available individually and in a set from NAEYC.

Through its publications program, the National Association for the Education of Young Children (NAEYC) provides a forum for discussion of major issues and ideas in the early childhood field, with the hope of provoking thought and promoting professional growth. The views expressed or implied in this book are not necessarily those of the Association or its members.

Carol Copple, *publications director*; Bry Pollack, *managing editor*; Malini Dominey, *design and production*; Cassandra Berman, *editorial associate*; Melissa Edwards, *editorial assistant*.

NAEYC Item #2012
ISBN: 978-1-928896-49-4

NAEYC Item #2013 (set)
ISBN: 978-1-928896-50-0 (set)

Contents

About This Book

This collection of stories, activities, discussion topics, and ideas for journaling has been written specifically to be used with the Special NAEYC Edition of Janet Gonzalez-Mena's book *Diversity in Early Care and Education: Honoring Differences*, 5th ed. (McGraw-Hill, 2008). We have been inventing activities for diversity training together since the early 1990s. This book contains both original activities that have proved successful over the years and activities borrowed and adapted, with credit given when we could recall.

We have addressed this companion resource to those who teach or train teachers and other early childhood practitioners who work with children and families in various early childhood settings. Teacher educators, trainers, consultants, and program directors will find its activities useful for professional development, whether in classes, staff meetings, or consultant work.[1] Many of the stories, questions, and self-reflection ideas can also be used by individual students, teachers, or practitioners for personal work, although we haven't addressed those audiences directly.

Practice in Building Bridges is loosely organized around the idea that by making further connections with information, examples, and stories through training and self-reflection, we all can become more self-aware, aware of others, and able to see where *antibias* work is needed to change environments and behaviors. Our ultimate goal is to swell the ranks of devoted antibias advocates prepared to make the changes in early care and education that will lead to greater equity and social justice in society.

> **"Antibias"**—An active/activist approach to challenging prejudice, stereotyping, bias, and the "isms." In a society in which institutional structures create and maintain sexism, racism, and handicappism, it is not sufficient to be nonbiased (and also highly unlikely), nor is it sufficient to be an observer. It is necessary for each individual to actively intervene, to challenge and counter the personal and institutional behaviors that perpetuate oppression.
>
> Source: L. Derman-Sparks and the A.B.C. Task Force. *Anti-Bias Curriculum: Tools for Empowering Young Children* (Washington, DC: NAEYC, 1989), p. 3.

Note

1. For those teachers and trainers who want to go further, an excellent training manual is *Bridging Cultures in Early Care and Education: A Training Module,* by M. Zepeda, J. Gonzalez-Mena, C. Rothstein-Fisch, and E. Trumbull (Erlbaum, 2006). *Practice in Building Bridges* in no way duplicates that manual, which is a result of several years work by the four authors on the Bridging Cultures Project at WestEd and grew out of a previous research project conducted by Patricia Greenfield of the University of California, Los Angeles.

Introduction to Building Bridges

We believe that people have to do their own work if they want to understand themselves better and grow. They can't expect to get "right" answers or easy solutions from a book or even from other people. Answers and solutions come only through interactions with others. So our approach to antibias advocacy emphasizes interactions and *transformative education*, which is what occurs when two people (or groups of people) come together and interact in such a way that both are changed.

The title *Practice in Building Bridges* represents our overarching goal in writing both this resource and the volume it supplements—**to help people create authentic, healthy, equitable relationships with people unlike themselves,** whether colleagues, coworkers, fellow students, or families of young children. The first step in that process involves focusing on one's own identity, perspectives, and reactions. Then it moves out from there to personal relationships and interactions, then to the environment, and finally to taking a stand. Mirroring that progression, we hope that doing the activities will help participants to:

Goal 1. Increase their self-awareness and understanding and feel good about who they are.

Goal 2. Increase their comfort level around people who are different from themselves through greater empathy and understanding.

Goal 3. Increase their ability to critically analyze environments and interactions, with an eye to expanding the antibias qualities in those contexts.

Goal 4. Become more able to stand up to injustice and find ways to make changes.[1]

Although this last goal is not written specifically into any of the activities that follow, we have found in our experience as trainers that by creating a space for authentic dialogue, participants reach not only the first three goals but also the fourth one. We approach antibias training by recognizing and honoring the humanity of each participant, without blaming, accusing, or attacking anybody. As participants reflect on their own cultural context, learn about others', and discover where inequity lies, they want to *do* something to change things.

Who We Are

In any diversity book, the personal is important—it's a vital part of *Diversity in Early Care and Education,* and so it is part of this companion resource, as well. In other words, although we wrote together, we also each wrote from our individual experiences and shared our own ideas and stories. One of our goals was to make sections of this book read like a conversation between friends from different cultures—one African American and one European American. So it matters who we are.

Intisar Shareef is professor and chair of the Early Childhood Department at Contra Costa College. The San Francisco Bay Area campus attracts a highly diverse student body—including African Americans, like herself, and many immigrants from all over. She teaches a full-time load plus directs several grants, one of which provides foster parent training. She has a doctorate in early childhood education from Nova University.

Janet Gonzalez-Mena is a retired community college teacher, who now writes and consults as an early childhood specialist. Her ancestral roots lie mostly in the British Isles, and she's a European American who knows she has a culture. She gained her double Spanish surname from her husband, who was born and raised in Mexico. She has a master's degree in human development from Pacific Oaks College.

Our relationship goes back about 26 years, when both of us were mothers of young children and involved in early childhood staff development. We met when Intisar hired Janet to do child development associate work in Head Start. Several years later we both ended up as

Head Start trainers in a project out of San Francisco State College. We have been friends ever since and started doing workshops and trainings together, mostly on diversity issues in early childhood education. We have presented in at least 10 different states and work regularly together in California.

Our relationship is important because it is an example of how two people have been practicing bridge building for a number of years in ways that let them learn about each other and work together to stand up to racism and the other "isms." This book comes partly from conversations we have had over the years, stories we have told each other, and a whole stack of letters we have exchanged. Here's a piece from a letter Intisar wrote to Janet in 2006 after doing a diversity presentation together in Boston. Intisar addressed Janet's concern that change is slow:

> "We're on this journey, and it's going to take a concerted effort for us to dismantle and reconstruct mindsets and institutions to truly facilitate freedom and equity. I think you and I represent an honest effort to tell our truths. . . . We all live in zones of alienation, clinging to our notions of either superiority or inferiority . . . our lenses color our world. Sometimes you and I wipe the lenses a bit, and we get an opportunity to peep to the other side. What would it look like if two women from very different experiences worked together collaboratively and explored the possibility of honoring the diversity of not only their lives but the lives of others? It's an interesting question, and we keep going at it with renewed interest and passion. So I'm never really worried, Janet, because we legitimately want to do this work. And if others are of like mind, they will recognize what we are doing, and we'll be that much further down the line."

To us, this excerpt represents the passion and dedication we two have to building bridges to cross cultures and create a more equitable society.

The Importance of Storytelling

Telling stories helps people gain personal insight and begin to construct a bridge across "otherness" to people who are different from them. A benefit of telling one's story and having others listen, accept, and tell their own is that we begin to define the human experience from a much broader perspective. Here's an example:

> Once there was a white woman who was hired to give parenting classes to a group of young African American women. As she was working with them, she heard a number of stories about their lives. She felt disconnected and inadequate because she was trying to teach them but realized how little her life touched theirs. She told Intisar her frustrations about trying to relate to them, and Intisar said, "They are telling you their stories; tell them your story." Ten years later, when she and Intisar came together at another

meeting, she told Intisar how useful that advice had been. Once she told her story, the connections started and opened up her work.

Today that woman is dedicated to equity, as she continues to learn more about herself and to share herself in ways that lead others to learn more about her. She used storytelling to reach the four goals we laid out at the beginning of this chapter. Reaching Goals 1 and 2 allowed her to move on to Goals 3 and 4.

Telling one's story in the effort to build bridges isn't about giving a lesson in what "right" looks like. It's an invitation for self-analysis and sharing so everyone feels free to speak about what they know. Those personal disclosures show bits and pieces of a larger picture, allowing us all to begin to see how things fit together and form the mosaic called human development. Intisar describes her own early stages of self-analysis and critique:

"It led me to many interesting encounters, from public displays of outrage to midnight intimate conversations with friends and family members."

Janet has her own story about Intisar's public displays of outrage over inequity:

"The first lesson I learned was that anger is an appropriate response to racism. Instead of getting defensive and protesting innocence, I would remind myself that anger over racism or any other oppression relates to a long, hard history that is a lot bigger and uglier than whatever recent event triggered that anger. I practiced feeling empathy and staying calm. And I began to notice that some white people responded to anger from people of color by getting angry back, arguing, trying to explain away the feelings, even changing the subject. I wondered, were they covering up feelings of guilt, even self-pity, perhaps? I saw what a difference it made if I just listened without trying to find the 'right' response. It was an important lesson for this white woman to learn—to just listen."

As all these examples show, storytelling is a powerful tool—one we use liberally in our professional work as trainers and throughout the activities that follow in this book. Having people tell their own story and listen to the stories of others, as they read through the chapters of *Diversity in Early Care and Education*, helps them become more comfortable with themselves and with people who are not like them. Reaching those first two goals begins building the bridge needed to move on to Goals 3 and 4.

Note
1. Adapted from the handout "Anti-Bias Curriculum Goals," copyrighted by Louise Derman-Sparks, 1992.

1

Perceiving and Responding to Differences

In *Diversity in Early Care and Education*, Chapter 1 is about the aspects that make up a person's "cultural framework" and the ways people from other cultural frameworks are different. The activity below is aimed at helping participants reflect on their own cultural framework and begin to explore frameworks different from theirs. The overall goal is to increase their self-awareness and positive aspects of self-identity, as well as gain empathy for those who are different.

Activity: *Personalized Name Tags*

One way to start participants telling each other stories is to have them create a name tag for themselves that includes a symbol or a picture of something that they feel proud about. Go around the room and have them all share their names and what they feel proud about.

Discussion Topics

1. Have them discuss Chapter 1's *Focus Questions* or the nine *Points to Ponder.* One way to do this is to have small groups or pairs pick either a Focus Question or a Point to Ponder to discuss, and then report back a highlight of the discussion to the larger group.

2. Either make a handout or read one (or both) of Our Stories on the next page aloud to the group. After reading the stories, put participants into pairs. Have them tell their own stories to each other and discuss their ideas, experiences, and feelings about the biases they learned growing up.

3. Early childhood professionals should "respect the dignity and preferences of each family and…make an effort to learn about its structure, culture, language, customs, and beliefs."[1] Create a discussion around the kinds of challenges and successes participants have had in working with diverse families.

Self-Reflection: *Journal Entry*

Ask participants to reflect on the following: "Describe your cultural framework using the *attributes of culture* (race, gender, age, etc.) that are listed in Chapter 1 (page 9). What attributes can you add to that list that have an influence on your life? How would you rank the attributes in order of their importance in *connecting* you with other people? In *separating* you from others?"

Note

1. *NAEYC Code of Ethical Conduct and Statement of Commitment.* A Position Statement of the National Association for the Education of Young Children (Washington, DC: Author, 2005), Ideal 2.5.

Our Stories

[Perceiving and Responding to Differences]

Intisar on income and class issues:

I'm reminded of how I triumphantly came home from college and announced to my family that we were "poor," according to the charts in my sociology textbook. I'll never forget the look on my father's face as he called me an "educated fool." How dare I cast him and my entire family into a socioeconomic level that belied my father's tireless efforts to keep his family middle class? He worked every day, paid a mortgage, provided for a wife and four children, took a vacation to Virginia every year, and made sure we were visited yearly by Santa Claus. How dare I overlook these efforts and categorize him as "poor." Economic income did not solely tell the story of who we were as a family. It obviously did not fit my father's characterization of himself.

Janet on growing up:

Income didn't tell the story of my family, either. We were poor, but we were proud. We were a "broken family" in those days, because my divorced mother took her two daughters and went home to her parents. There were five to seven of us in the house (my uncles also lived there periodically). We lived mostly on my grandfather's meager pension. We would have been a Head Start family if there had been such a thing back then. We lived in a two-bedroom, one-bathroom hundred-year-old house that had once belonged to my grandmother's aunt. The house, which had been in the family for many years, was in a mixed-income neighborhood, with some larger one-family homes and a number of small low-income apartments. I was carefully taught to be a classist and to put myself above people who didn't talk like we did and didn't share the same manners. I'm still discovering and dealing with attitudes in me that get in the way of my equity work!

2

Communicating Across Cultures

In *Diversity in Early Care and Education*, Chapter 2 is about cross-cultural communication skills. The activity below is intended to help participants experience differences in communication as well as practice suspending judgment about styles of communication that are different from theirs. The overall goal is to increase their comfort level in cross-cultural encounters.

Activity: *Mingling*

Ask participants to stand up and move around the room, introducing themselves to another person, telling that person one thing about themselves, hearing one thing about the other person, and then moving on to talk to someone new. Stop them periodically and ask them to notice aspects of communication, which can differ markedly across cultures.

Ask them to notice, for example, how close they are standing when they are chatting (*personal space*). Suggest that they try violating their partner's personal space by coming too close. Ask them to distance themselves, and ask how that feels. In a bit, stop them and have them talk to their partner about eye contact—what feels comfortable? What doesn't? How much do they notice facial expressions? What does smiling tell them? Does the other person use hand gestures or not? Stop them again. How much is touching a part of communication? How does each partner feel about periods of silence during a conversation? How did time factors influence this communication experience?

Finally, ask them to read the section "Learning to Communicate Across Cultures" (Chapter 2, pages 34–39) and discuss how that reading related to their experience of the exercise.

Discussion Topics

1. Have participants discuss Chapter 2's *Focus Questions* or the four *Points to Ponder.* One way to do this is to have small groups or pairs pick either a Focus Question or a Point to Ponder to discuss, and then report back a highlight of the discussion to the larger group.

2. Either make a handout or read one (or both) of Our Stories on the next two pages aloud to the group. After reading the stories, put participants into pairs. Have them tell each other their own stories about cross-cultural or cross-gender communication.

Self-Reflection: *Journal Entry*

Ask participants to reflect on the following: "What experiences have you had in communicating across cultures? What do you find most difficult in cross-cultural communication? How is communicating across genders like or different from communicating across cultures?"

Our Stories

[Communicating Across Cultures]

Intisar as a community college practicum teacher:

I remember a very interesting story that a preschool director shared with me. It was a turning point for her, as she recalls "getting it" for the first time that a view seemingly contrary from the standard early childhood education culture might have merit and be worth considering as a viable alternative.

The staff at her center seemed concerned that a female child of Middle Eastern descent had low self-esteem. They saw her as retiring, passive, not as autonomous and assertive as they perceived she could or should be. The staff presented their concerns to the director with documentation from observations to support their analysis. The director decided to meet with the parents and focus her discussion on how important it is to notice and praise children for their efforts and accomplishments. After a few roundabout exchanges, the director decided to be more forthright, and she directly asked the parents, "Well, do you praise your daughter for anything?"

The parents were very reserved as they looked at each other. And then one responded, "We praise Allah. We love our daughter."

The director was completely surprised but had the wherewithal to ask the parents to explain. Given this opening, a very healthy discussion ensued, where the parents felt invited and enabled to tell their story about how they viewed praise and why they considered praise to be reserved for God. They confidently expressed their love for their child, and a transformation of opinions occurred on both sides. This ability to find common ground on behalf of the child occurred because parents felt compelled to tell "their truth" in the face of "the authority"; and the authority figure allowed herself to become a "student" of the parents.

Janet as a trainer:

Among the times I have done the Mingling exercise—where participants walk around and interact while being aware of such things as how close they stand—a particular incident stands out. There was a woman from a country outside the United States who stood so close to the people she talked with that they felt uncomfortable. At the end of the exercise, some people expressed their feelings about their space having been invaded by this woman. She was surprised. When someone commented that her proximity patterns were based in her culture, she strongly denied any cultural influence. She said that she was just a friendly person, and that was the way she showed it. She also complained that people who backed away from her advances were "cold people—standoffish." It wasn't until she researched her own culture that she finally decided that maybe it really was a cultural difference.

I remember, myself, how it feels to have someone invade my personal space. A woman from India had a long conversation with me once in a crowded room. I don't know what her culture was, as there are many different cultures in India. She was trying to convince me to do something I didn't want to do—I've forgotten now what it was. She kept getting closer and closer to me, until she was "in my face," as the expression goes. I kept moving away, until I discovered she had backed me into a corner. I was aware at the time of feeling trapped, though I'm sure she would have been surprised to hear that I felt that way.

3

Working with
Diversity Issues

In *Diversity in Early Care and Education*, Chapter 3 looks at examples of what can be called cultural "bumps"; for example, when teachers and parents don't see eye to eye. The chapter also explains a process for negotiating the bumps in ways that satisfy everybody involved. The activity below has participants actually role playing the scenarios and practicing the skills explained in the chapter. An overall goal is to help participants explore their ability to make a critical analysis of interactions in order to expand the antibias qualities in those interactions.

Activity: *Role Play*

Have participants read Chapter 3's three scenarios. Then choose pairs to role play a discussion between the adults involved in the scenarios, while the rest of the group watches. Let the pair role play each scene any way they want the first time. The second time, make the role play into a listening exercise, and have the participants playing the "teachers" practice their listening skills by just listening and responding nonverbally. Tell them, "Don't ask questions or say anything, just listen." The point is to really hear the other person's perspective and not judge it. The third time, make the role play into a chance to practice the RERUN process, which is explained in Chapter 3 on pages 58–60.

Discussion Topics

1. Have participants discuss Chapter 3's *Focus Questions* or the four *Points to Ponder*. One way to do this is to have small groups or pairs pick either a Focus Question or a Point to Ponder to discuss, and then report back a highlight of the discussion to the larger group.

2. Either make a handout or read one (or both) of Our Stories on the next page aloud to the group. After reading the stories, put participants into pairs. Have them tell their own stories to each other about being a parent, or being a teacher, and working with someone whose perspectives differed from their own.

Self-Reflection: *Journal Entry*

Ask participants to reflect on the following: "Consider this quote by Rumi: *Out beyond ideas of right doing and wrong doing lies a field—I'll meet you there.* If you were to meet someone out there in that field, whom might it be? What would you perceive your differences to be? Construct a RERUN dialogue between you and that other person, in which you practice the RERUN process to discuss your differences. Focus more on understanding the other person and gaining insights into where you got your perspective, than on resolving the differences."

R=reflect
E=explain
R=reason
U=understand
N=negotiate

Our Stories

[Working with Diversity Issues]

Intisar as a parent:

Parenting has not been easy for me as the adoptive, single parent of three male children, two of whom are extremely challenging. I've had to use the wisdom of my ancestors, the insight of early childhood best practice, and some concoctions I made up on the spur of the moment, in order to get me through the daily dilemmas. As I look back, I value all of the above because they have made me the person I am today, and I continue to marvel at me as I re-create myself daily. This is the gift I wish to give every educator and parent: the gift of imperfection and creativity. We have a plethora of tools and ideas to pull from. Enjoy the luxury and benefits of living in a multicultural society that allows us to learn from so many resources. I'm so enriched by the experiences of others.

Janet as an early childhood educator:

Parenting wasn't exactly easy for me, either. (Is it easy for anybody?) But for a period I felt secure in the knowledge that I knew what to do, even if I didn't always do it. When I was finally fully qualified as an early childhood education teacher, I was really a know-it-all and readily argued with anybody who tried to disagree with me. I thought my way was the right way, and though I was polite, I didn't really try to understand other points of view. It took a number of cultural bumps for me to begin to understand that my perspective is shaped by my culture and that there is plenty of room in our field for a variety of perspectives, culturally shaped and otherwise.

4

A Framework for Understanding Differences

In *Diversity in Early Care and Education*, Chapter 4 looks at two different basic orientations—*individualist* and *collectivist*—and explores how these different orientations affect care and education practices. The activity involves getting beneath the surface of rationality to look at one's own hot buttons or sore spots. The second part of the activity involves sharing personal issues in ways that create honest, authentic exchanges with people whose frameworks are different. An overall goal is to help participants explore their ability to make a critical analysis of interactions in order to expand the antibias qualities in those interactions.

Activity: *Quick Write & Share*

Introduce the activity by saying something like the following:

> Being culturally responsive means you have to look inside yourself and explore your own culture, including feelings and experiences. The care aspect of early care and education is a good place to look for cultural differences, because they often show up there. This self-reflective exercise has two purposes: To help you focus inward and then to share what you discover with someone who isn't particularly like you.

Using the questions below, have participants do a "quick write"—that is, jotting down notes in answer to the questions. Then have them form pairs and share with each other what they wrote, and then report back what they gained from the activity.

Interview Questions

1. When you think about the various essential activities of daily living (e.g., eating and mealtimes, toileting and toilet training, grooming, washing, bathing, sleeping), what associations, memories, feelings, or experiences come to your mind? Consider group associations, modern as well as historical, along with looking at your own personal associations.

2. Do you have some issues around any of these essential activities of daily living? Do you have blind spots, hot buttons, or particular perspectives related to these activities? If yes, of what importance or significance are these to your work with children, families, or staff?

3. How does your discussion of your feelings or issues better prepare you to work with children, families, or staff?

Discussion Topics

1. Have participants discuss Chapter 4's *Focus Questions* or the five *Points to Ponder.* One way to do this is to have small groups or pairs pick either a Focus Question or a Point to Ponder to discuss, and then report back a highlight of the discussion to the larger group.

2. Either make a handout or read one (or both) of Our Stories on the next two pages aloud to the group. Then put participants into pairs. Have them tell their own stories of tensions related to independence and interdependence. They can also consider the tensions that might arise when a teacher with a strong priority for independence is working with a mother who wants her child spoon-fed.

Self-Reflection: *Journal Entry*

Ask participants to reflect on the following: "Think about what you learned from reading Chapter 4 and the discussions about the framework of independence/interdependence.[1] How much do you believe this framework relates to cultural differences? Did you gain any insights about your own culture? Any insights about another culture?"[2]

Notes

1. You can use the training module *Bridging Cultures in Early Care and Education* to help participants explore this framework in depth.

2. The Self-Reflection can be followed up by having participants read the beginning section of Chapter 7, "Differing Goals of Socialization" (pages 125–127), which looks at some other possible aspects of differing cultural priorities.

Our Stories

[A Framework for Understanding Differences]

Intisar on notions of independence and interdependence:

Thinking about my family and the messages I received, I remember the story of my grandfather's escape "up north." I've heard similar stories about the migration of black people from the South to the North. What's often similar in these stories is the substory about how folks in previous generations had to depend on each other as they sojourned. People lived with each other in close quarters; there were shared meals, caring for each other's children, finding jobs for self and others. My father and mother spent the early years of their marriage in extended family units, living with my paternal grandparents, later buying a two-family house with a cousin, and finally purchasing another two-family house (duplex) and renting out one unit. However, I can remember how my father longed for a single-family dwelling—I believe, because he thought that was the ultimate expression of success, a man who could provide "a house" for his family.

African Americans of my generation who were successful in school moved away from our black community. If you were successful and smart, why would you remain in the ghetto? If you had the ability to get up out of there and move away—especially to a white neighborhood, which represented success—then you owed it to yourself and your family to do so. That gave your parents "bragging rights." That is, that even if *they* were stuck in the ghetto, they had been smart enough to get their kids out. Interdependence was seen as something negative, like you couldn't do anything better or you couldn't get out so you were stuck in the black neighborhood with the rest of the "losers." When I moved from the East to California, it was seen in my family as a big sign of success.

Decades later, after my mother died and all the children had moved from our family home, my father decided to purchase a home with his aging brothers and sisters. He had remained connected to his roots and the notion of interdependence, and those family connections gave him solace at the end of his life. I reflect on this message because this feeling of interdependence is very strong in me, and I've constructed a "family" from the people I've met here in California and the children I've adopted.

I also value my independence and the strength that I've gained from my ability to incorporate identity and imitate European American middle-class values—*when in Rome, do as the Romans do.* But I don't value or worship one way over the other. I honor and marvel in my ability to benefit from both. I truly appreciate the education I have and my capabilities as an educator, but I know my strength lies in my ability to reach back and hold onto the "mother wit" and cultural connections I received from my parents and my childhood community. My commitment is to pass that message on to others, so we *never* feel that we must choose to be this *or* that. We are *all* of that.

Janet on the subject of independence and interdependence:

Both sets of my grandparents as young couples left their families and moved far away to settle in another state. They struck out on their own and raised their children on their own. Independence was a strong priority, and dependence was something to be avoided. As fate would have it, my mother ended up as a single parent and became dependent on her parents. I didn't question any of this at the time. But growing up, I knew the ideal was to have your own home and live in a nuclear family. My mother, when she finally got a job that paid enough for us to move out, became fiercely independent and made it clear to her daughters that she never intended to be dependent on anybody again.

I took seriously the idea of making independence a top priority in rearing my children. As a mother of mostly males, I was careful not to create any "mama's boys." As a result, my sons from my first marriage aren't nearly as close to me as my last son, who came much later, from my marriage to my current husband, who grew up in a large, interdependent family in Mexico. When that son was young, my husband and I had many arguments over our differences, but not nearly as many as I had with my mother-in-law. It took me a long time to realize that her interdependent child-rearing style worked well. Certainly my husband had turned out great—able to create close relationships but also be amazingly independent! I didn't realize this until after my mother-in-law had died. So partly, I'm in this diversity work as an apology to her for being so blind and stubborn!

5

Attachment and Separation

In *Diversity in Early Care and Education*, Chapter 5 narrows the focus on the individualist and collectivist frameworks to explore how they affect attachment and separation issues. The activity below helps participants relate to how a parent might feel leaving a child in the care of another person. The overall goal is to foster more empathic relationships between teachers and families.

Activity: *Precious Object Exercise*[1]

Tell participants to choose something important to them from among the items they have with them—some valued object that says something about them, an item they can hold in their hand. Once everyone has chosen, tell them that this is a listening exercise, and *without talking,* to pair up with someone they don't know or don't know well. Have the pairs exchange objects, and decide who will be the *talker* and who will be the *listener*. Explain the rules:

- Talkers, say why the object is important to you and what it says about you.
- Listeners, you must listen without talking. No questions, comments, or discussion. Indicate nonverbally that you are listening.
- The talker has two minutes to explain, and then you will switch roles.
- Objects are to remain in the hands of the other person until you tell them to give them back.

After everyone has had a chance to be both talker and listener, ask, "What if I told you that the other person would be holding your object until the end of today? How would you feel? What if I told you that when you get your object back, it won't be quite the same because the person holding it will have established her own relationship with it?"

Be silent for a moment to let participants react. Usually there is a wave of emotions. What are they feeling? What was their experience of this exercise? What came up for them? Usually someone mentions that the exercise is something like parents leaving a child in a program with a teacher they don't know or don't know very well. Cultural and language differences sometimes come up. Be sure the following points are covered if they don't come out naturally in the discussion:

- Families are entrusting their most precious thing when they leave their child in a care and education program.
- A family goes through a significant letting-go process in allowing teachers to establish a relationship with their child.
- Trust issues can cause tension, discomfort, or stress.

Discussion Topics

1. Have participants discuss Chapter 5's *Focus Questions* or the five *Points to Ponder*. Alternatively, you could have the whole group discuss *boundary issues* after reading Point to Ponder 5.2 (on page 91).

2. Either make a handout or read one (or both) of Our Stories on the next two pages aloud to the group. Then put participants into pairs. Have them tell their own attachment and separation stories to each other.

Self-Reflection: *Journal Entry*

Ask participants to reflect on the following: "What does the term *cutting the apron strings* mean to you? Anthropologist Edward T. Hall says the world is divided into those cultures that cut the apron strings and those that do not. Do you buy that idea? What are your own experiences, ideas, and feelings about attachment?"

Alternatively: "What do you know about the history of your family and life-threats to their babies? What about life-threats to older children? Do you see a connection between life-threats and child-rearing practices in your family of origin?"

Note

1. Thanks to Gretchen Brooke, retired faculty, Pacific Oaks College, for this idea.

Shareef & Gonzalez-Mena

Our Stories

[Attachment and Separation]

Intisar on redefining "family":

When Janet and I began our discussion about attachment, I found myself reflecting on my relationship with my three adopted sons. I have been challenged in so many ways to rethink and review my stereotypical ideas about how children attach to their parents and caregivers. Attachment is a lifelong process. It's true that the initial stages of attachment are formed in infancy, but my experience has taught me that children and adults are constantly renegotiating attachment relationships throughout the lifespan. While attachment to parents or parent substitutes may be very significant, I want to acknowledge the importance of attachment to the group or collective.

I work with foster parents and the foster care system. I see some of the positive outcomes of this system, but am often dismayed by its flaws. I think the history of African Americans gives us some clues about alternatives. Historically, foster care was not necessarily an option. African American children whose parents didn't or couldn't take care of them were instead raised by the collective. This might be a relative, or a non-relative. The children were taken in by others who lived in the community and were often somehow connected to the family of origin. So they were never too far away from their roots—they were readily absorbed into the kinship network. Folks often couldn't explain how the child they were raising was related to them; but few people asked for an explanation. So-and-so was just "family," and that was the end of it.

I tell this story as a way of reminding us that we come from a history that has rich lessons to teach us about what "family" can mean. Two of my sons (teenagers now) have made attempts to construct family from an assortment of "others" I sometimes deem as less desirable. I've had to rethink some of my prejudgments as I witness the benefits that accrue from their attachment to youths who share their stories and others who are sympathetic and knowledgeable about their realities. I've had to admit that I'm ignorant about my children's circumstances and feelings and allow myself to become a listener and learner instead of an "authority." Typically, this change of posture allows for a healing to occur.

Janet on attachment:

When I was a teenager, my mother struck out on her own, leaving her parents and taking her two daughters. We moved to a small community three hours away from my grandparents—the family I had been part of from first through eighth grade. I was so lonely! I remember hiding in the bathroom and crying. I was in a new school, in a new community, and felt so insecure. But then I did what I've since seen other teens do—I adopted a family, that of my boyfriend.

Looking back, I think that my relationship with his family was more important to me than my relationship with him. I was a daughter to his parents and a big sister to his siblings. I spent a lot of time in their home. That family got me through my first two years of high school, and then they moved far away. I don't remember their leaving as being a big jolt—they filled a need in me just at the right time. In another two years, when I finished high school, I was feeling much more secure and was ready to move on. By then, leaving home (and my mother and sister) wasn't nearly as hard as it had been to leave my grandparents and the childhood security of knowing where I belonged.

6

Differing Perspectives on Learning through Play

In *Diversity in Early Care and Education*, Chapter 6 focuses on play, a timely and highly emotional subject in the early care and education field. Disagreements abound about *play* as a learning experience, not only between parents and teachers but also among early childhood professionals themselves. The chapter explores diverse views of play. The activity below is designed to help participants avoid taking sides, by exploring the value of play and examining cultural messages children learn from a variety of play activities. The overall goal is to move beyond either/or views and find common ground, because operating on common ground is a way of increasing equity.

Activity: *Give-One, Get-One Exercise*

Have participants crease a sheet of paper into halves lengthwise. At the top in the left half, have them write the heading "Give-One" then number down the left edge of the paper ("1, 2, 3, 4,...") all the way to the bottom of the sheet. Then in the right half, have them write at the top "Get-One" then number again ("1, 2, 3, 4,..."), along the crease, to the bottom of the sheet. Then, say:

> Think about how you played as a child. Now, under the heading "Give-One," next to the first three numbers, write down three ways you played as a child— things you did that stick out in your memory. When you have written down

your three, approach someone else and give that person one of your ideas. Write down one of that person's ideas in the "Get-One" column, writing the person's name down next to the idea. Move around the room until you have given three of your ideas and received at least six new ideas, writing down the owner's name with each.

After the mingling, ask everyone to be seated. Start things off by selecting someone to read an idea from her "Get-One" column, then asking the person who *gave* her that idea to stand and describe the play and what he got out of it. The sharing can be extended and related to Chapter 6 with the following questions: "Did you learn anything from the play? Were there any cultural implications; that is, was what you did more object-oriented or people-oriented, for example?"

When that person finishes describing and talking about the play, he chooses an item off his "Get-One" list and calls the name of the person who gave him that idea. She then reports to the group...and so on. Depending on the size of the group, the activity continues until all or at least most people have been called. The reflection and discussion afterward can focus on what participants got out of the activity.

Another point to make is that there was a difference between the way the people who shared were chosen in this activity and how they would usually be chosen: by the teacher/trainer, by participants raising their hands, or by them competing for the floor. In this activity, did some people speak who ordinarily would not have?

Discussion Topics

1. Have participants discuss Chapter 6's *Focus Questions* or the six *Points to Ponder*. One way to do this is to have small groups or pairs pick either a Focus Question or a Point to Ponder to discuss, and then report back a highlight of the discussion to the larger group.

2. Either make a handout or read one (or both) of Our Stories on the following two pages aloud to the group. Then put participants into pairs. Have them tell their own stories to each other, centered on their experiences with tensions related to differing perspectives on play. They can also consider the tensions that might arise when a teacher with a strong priority for play as learning, for example, is working with a parent who has a different perspective, or vice versa.

Self-Reflection: *Journal Entry*

Ask participants to reflect on the following: "What do you remember about playing? Where did you play? Mostly outdoors, mostly indoors, or both? If you played outdoors, where were you most likely to play? Were you allowed to play alone, or were you supervised? What games did you play? What did you learn? Did you have play activities that weren't games? What were they? How did your play affect your way of looking at interactions with others? Do you see ideas of independence or interdependence embodied in these early play experiences? Was there something cultural about the way you played or the way your play was regarded by adults? Do you see any implications for learning in indoor play? In outdoor play?"

Our Stories

[Differing Perspectives on Learning through Play]

Intisar on play as connecting:

Parents and early childhood practitioners of color often have confused feelings about the role of play. I think that in the African American culture, *playing* signifies "having a good time" and "socially interacting," more than it does "engaging in a learning experience" as such. Initially, I myself had a hard time incorporating how play could be beneficial to academic achievement. Achievement is important in Western society, and people of color often see the need to push achievement just so our children can be seen as average. This concept of young children of color getting a strong start is not a new idea. Play was not on the minds of the early childhood educators who saw the need to establish the Mississippi Freedom Schools; liberation was the goal. Today, things remain pretty much the same way.

I think we need to think more about a *both/and* proposition, rather than an *either/or*. There is value in both play and achievement. So much of our experience as African Americans centers around social engagement and personal interaction. We often find our empowerment and our solace in our connections, so it's easy to understand how our children might gravitate more toward the engaged, social interactions of play rather than the solitary, nonengagement of some abstract learning activities.

What I fondly recall from my childhood is playing hide-and-seek indoors with my siblings and mother (my father was working overtime, and my mother took liberties when he was not there). These moments of intense pleasure brought me closer to my family and made my sheltered life exciting. I also remember playing hide-and-seek outdoors in the summer; overcoming fears of darkness and being caught were a big payoff from that game.

What was memorable was the delight of playing together, whether jacks, jump rope, tag, or Monopoly. It really didn't take much for us to feel good about what we were doing. It just felt good doing it together.

I still feel that intense pleasure of belonging when I go to a party or gathering and folks begin to laugh and dance. The sense of connection heightens my awareness and seems to make me more conscious of what's going on around me. I believe children who are field-sensitive need the social interactions associated with play to help stimulate their learning receptivity. Being forced to function in a sterile, impersonal, and individualistically oriented learning environment or interest center can be an alien experience for children who are used to an adult lap to crawl onto or siblings who sit near and coax them through an unfamiliar task. Asking questions to find out how and what children play at home may be an illuminating experience for a teacher.

Janet's memory of playing:

I loved what I now know as "dramatic play" or "playing pretend." I didn't need much to make up whole scenarios and play them out. Sometimes I had a playmate, but often I played by myself. Sometimes it was playing House; but other times, the imaginary settings and actions were more dramatic. I remember as an adult trying to write a novel. The feeling I got while I was writing was very much like when playing pretend as a child. I remember once writing about a winter scene. I was at my desk in front of the window. I don't remember what was happening in the story, but the setting felt very real. I was astonished to look out the window after half an hour of intensive writing and discover it was the middle of summer. That's how deeply I'm able to concentrate when entering my imagination—even as an adult. I don't know if I'm unusual or not. I never talked about this with anybody.

7

Socialization, Guidance, and Discipline

In *Diversity in Early Care and Education*, Chapter 7 focuses on socialization, particularly on what is perhaps the hottest topic in the early childhood field today: what professionals call *guidance* and families typically call *discipline*. Issues such as inner controls, power, and authority are topics of the chapter. As always, our approach is to encourage interactions among participants as a way of practicing building bridges. This last activity is another opportunity to share lived experiences, but in a project involving symbols. This shifts the group dynamics, giving space to participants who can express themselves graphically. In our experience, what often happens is that those who have been quiet when the modality was verbal now take leadership roles. The outcome of the activity is not so much in what shows on the paper, but the *process* of producing it. Again, the overall goal is to move beyond either/or views and find common ground as a way of increasing equity.

Activity: *Group Graphic*

In this activity, participants will draw *protection symbols*—graphical designs of special significance thought to protect one from harm. In her story, Intisar talks about the Hen's Foot, which for her captures her mother's disciplinary style in protecting and making her into a person strong enough to stand up to injustice. For Janet, protection was only a small part of how she was raised; discipline was more about socialization into a society that wasn't particularly dangerous. Interestingly, the "growth" symbol (the spiral shown here) that Janet has carried for many years turns out to also be an Irish protection symbol.

Have participants think back to their childhoods, to the discipline styles of their main caregivers. Now have them each draw a protection symbol—either one they know about or one they make up—that says something about that discipline style. After everyone has drawn an individual symbol, put participants into small groups with markers and chart paper to figure out a design that incorporates all their individual symbols into a group graphic.

Discussion Topics

1. Either make a handout or read one (or both) of Our Stories on the next two pages aloud to the group. Then have participants review the section "Misunderstandings" (Chapter 1, pages 18–19), about European American, Chinese, and African American cultural perspectives on parenting styles. Then put participants into pairs and have them discuss the parenting styles of their family of origin and their feelings about those styles.

2. Have participants discuss Chapter 7's *Focus Questions* or the three *Points to Ponder.* One way to do this is to have small groups or pairs pick either a Focus Question or a Point to Ponder to discuss, and then report back a highlight of the discussion to the larger group.

3. Discuss as a group Intisar's story specifically. Ask them: "Do most middle-class European American families have the same need to protect their children that Intisar's mother had? What special challenges might the families of African American males face? Families raising children in violence-prone communities? Immigrant families from war-torn countries? Families of girls, in the face of marketplace and media sexism and female sexualization? Families of children with exceptionalities?"

Self-Reflection: *Journal Entry*

Ask participants to reflect on the following: "How do you feel about the approaches to guidance and discipline used in your family of origin? Would/do you use those same approaches with children as a parent, potential parent, or teacher? Why or why not?"

Our Stories

[Socialization, Guidance, and Discipline]

Intisar on parenting styles:

As an early childhood instructor, the "parenting styles" lecture always made me queasy, because I felt a certain sense of disloyalty labeling my mother as "authoritarian" with all the negative consequences visited upon her children. My mother's parenting style didn't fit what I was teaching. Like many black women of her era, my mother was strong-willed, tough, loyal, and loving. I would later find out in reading about parenting that the preferred style—called "authoritative"—was based on the model of *independence,* where it's expected that children develop an internal locus of control at an early age. This fits in well with the theories of self-esteem, initiative, autonomy, and individuality.

It's one perspective, but is often perpetuated as the epitome of what it means to be human. While autonomy and the rest are highly regarded values in Western culture, 70 percent of the world's population tends to value *interdependence* as the higher priority.[1] For many cultures, survival depends on people living collectively and valuing the group more than the individual. Group esteem, supporting others, and respect for authority form the cornerstone of many cultures and families. Children in such cultures are taught at an early age to pay attention to adult cues, which govern their behavior. The locus of control is external, then becomes more internalized at a later age. Even as young adults, group members will defer to the elders and follow their directions. This notion of an external locus of control can be witnessed when a parent or elder gives "the look" to control the child's behavior. Many times children don't attend to adult vocalizations until they sense the adult means what he or she says. Direct commands, rather than open-ended questions, are what the child is familiar with.

Often people who are unfamiliar with cultural differences judge these differences as deficits and unfairly identify the parents or other adult figures who are more directive as being "punitive," "harsh," or "unfeeling." Thus, I felt the "authoritarian" parenting style, as described in most textbooks, missed who my mom really was—what she represented in my life.

It wasn't until I traveled to Ghana, West Africa, that I was able to "see" and embrace the parenting style I was familiar with. The Ghanaians have a system of symbols, called *Adrinka,* which are similar to Chinese characters. Each symbol represents a consciousness or value. I became

 enamored with the symbol called the Hen's Foot. The value represented in this symbol is maternal wisdom, patience, and strength. The literal translation of the symbol is: "The hen steps on her chicks, but does not kill them." When I read that sentence, my whole face lit up. Here was my mother captured in a symbol and a sentence. I had to come all the way to Africa to find her. However, where else would she be? It made all the sense in the world that I could identify with what I read. I am an African, and the information I need about myself, my culture, and my practices should come from my ancestors and my elders.

Again, I was enlightened and empowered by this knowledge. I've shared this information numerous times in workshops and classes, and the response is incredible. Women of color especially look up, smile, nod their heads, and frequently call out, "Amen." They recognize what I recognized. We are powerful people who have been the nurturers of many, our own offspring and those of others. Many presidents, leaders, and so-called successful and prominent individuals have found their strength and well-being in the bosom or on the shoulder or hip of an African American mother hen who was not afraid to step on "her" brood.

Janet on discipline as a preschool teacher:

I learned the lessons well of how to gently, quietly guide children's behavior in the preschool classroom. I thought I was pretty good at it until once during a staff meeting, a fellow teacher brought up the issue of the children for whom our "professional guidance styles" didn't work. She questioned whether, with our soft voices and unemotional approaches, some children never even heard us—or at least, if they did, they didn't pay attention. Later on, at an NAEYC annual conference, I attended a workshop by Janice Hale-Benson, an African American educator and writer. She talked about the "sweetie, sweetie, talky, talky" style of guidance. Although we had never met, I knew it was my style she was talking about.

Her point was that when that style doesn't work, children, especially African American children, run wild and end up being labeled as "problem" children. That really struck home with me, and I began to understand that there was a lot I didn't know, in spite of my education and degrees!

Note

1. H.C. Triandis. 1989. Cross-cultural studies of individualism and collectivism. *Nebraska Symposium on Motivation* 37:43–133.

Early years are learning years

Become a member of NAEYC, and help make them count!

Just as you help young children learn and grow, the National Association for the Education of Young Children—your professional organization—supports you in the work you love. NAEYC is the world's largest early childhood education organization, with a national network of local, state, and regional Affiliates. We are more than 100,000 members working together to bring high-quality early learning opportunities to all children from birth through age eight.

Since 1926, NAEYC has provided educational services and resources for people working with children, including:

• *Young Children*, the award-winning journal (six issues a year) for early childhood educators

• **Books, posters, brochures, and videos** to support your work with young children and families

• **The NAEYC Annual Conference**, which brings tens of thousands of people together from across the country and around the world to share their expertise and ideas on the education of young children

• **Insurance plans** for members and programs

• **A voluntary accreditation system** to help programs reach national standards for high-quality early childhood education

• **Young Children International** to promote global communication and information exchanges

• **www.naeyc.org**—a dynamic Web site with up-to-date information on all of our services and resources

To join NAEYC

To find a complete list of membership benefits and options or to join NAEYC online, visit **www.naeyc.org/membership.** Or you can mail this form to us.
(Membership must be for an individual, not a center or school.)

Name_____

Address_____

City_____State_____ ZIP _____

E-mail_____

Phone (H)_____(W)_____

❐ New member   ❐ Renewal ID #_____
Affiliate name/number_____

To determine your dues, you must visit www.naeyc.org/membership or call 800-424-2460, ext. 2002.

Indicate your payment option

❐ VISA ❐ MasterCard ❐ AmEx ❐ Discover

Card #_____ Exp. date _____

Cardholder's name _____

Signature_____

Note: By joining NAEYC you also become a member of your state and local Affiliates.

Send this form and payment to

NAEYC,
PO Box 97156
Washington, DC 20090-7156